PRAISE FOR *NIGHTFALL MARGINALIA*

"Sarah Maclay's dream-voice hums with the energy of heart-body desire and cleanses with the fineness of an excellent mind. These new poems feel gathered from the margins of a night continuously falling, shaped by an intimate twilit voice, starred with mythic images, that speak-sings in many registers. A narrative emerges, centering in a feminine figure both unique and representative of a city and a time. Yet there is no self-mythologizing here. Rather, the poet's voice discovers itself already within a mythic role in the here and now."
—JAMES CUSHING

"Finding beauty at the frayed edges of a collapsing world, Maclay's *Nightfall Marginalia* is a voluptuous enactment of both a ruminative intuition and an exuberant intelligence. A place to revel, where the fruit is heavy on the vine, each line a velvet cloak to be pulled up—to reveal the mysteries of desire, mortality, the nature(s) of consciousness itself. Blissfully, there are no easy answers here, just a deepening of the questions. One of contemporary poetry's most compelling sensualists, this is Maclay at the height of her bewitching powers."
—LOUISE MATHIAS

WHAT BOOKS PRESS

AN IMPRINT OF

THE GLASS TABLE

COLLECTIVE

LOS ANGELES

NIGHTFALL
MARGINALIA

NIGHTFALL
MARGINALIA

SARAH MACLAY

WHAT
BOOKS
PRESS

LOS ANGELES

Library of Congress Cataloging-in-Publication Data

Names: Maclay, Sarah, author.
Title: Nightfall marginalia / Sarach Maclay.
Description: Los Angeles : What Books Press, [2023] | Summary: "This book
   of nocturnes and ekphrastics--twilit, autumnal, narrowly perched between
   elegy, eros, prayer and grimoire--abandons diurnal constraint to embrace
   a poetry of dream"-- Provided by publisher.
Identifiers: LCCN 2023024910 | ISBN 9798986625829 (paperback)
Subjects: LCGFT: Poetry.
Classification: LCC PS3563.A317974 N54 2023 | DDC 811/.54--dc23/eng/2023
LC record available at https://lccn.loc.gov/2023024910

Cover art: Gronk, *Untitled*, mixed media on paper, 2022
Book design by ash good, www.ashgood.com

What Books Press
363 South Topanga Canyon Boulevard
Topanga, CA 90290

WHATBOOKSPRESS.COM

CONTENTS

The color of truth is gray.

—André Gide

THE GLASS SONATA

You called it something like thinking.

Let's say it was primarily a mode of transport,
      like a train.

That it moved smoothly.

Was transparent.

That we could see the details
      of the women's dresses,
        as they smoothed their hands—

        over twill, or silk,
        cotton, wool.

That the surface was as phallic
      as a monorail.

Or you could use it like a bullet—
      to slip in your jacket pocket
      just for touch—

      that is, remember
      what it's meant to do.

But this is a slipperier invention.

Even in the absence of muscle tone—
      still, the insisting flame.

The way it demands to make itself known—

to lead to what cannot be followed.

Here, it demands that we give up
 the beginning—not look back.

There could be words about the sound
of the fountain

or the small, concentric rings of light
as, late, they fall on paper.

But, really, that's not it.

Is it?

It's closer, even.
Closer to the body.

Here, we abandon years of insistent rhythm—
        just to hear it.
        But not its sound.

Can we be quiet enough together now
        to hear it—

        hear it
        and not break it—

THE SLEEPING ARROWS

The isle of rose, the river as wolf, a guilt-ripple
of wind—they come to me,

these gifts of misperception.

The tips are lead or gold,
in random order.

And nothing bothers my life
but the sense that it doesn't actually occur.

(In literal sleep, the pillow was strong and cold.
The hand was limp.

The tongue: asleep in the mouth.
No point in teeth.)

The commentator notes the supreme
innocence of the child's face—as he lets the arrows sail,

the lack of guile
or even intention.

(Someone had given me a candle
in a vintage-labeled jar: Defender Brand Tomatoes.

But, really, there was nothing to defend.)

Then I see my shadow
is the shadow of a stranger.

(In the literal world, the arrowheads
were damaging, and stone.)

Then I see my shadow
close the door.

Bleached and saturated white,
divided by a moving frame.

      ~

It would be as though a you
could speak.

SONG OF THE BROKEN DICE

It was then that I quit bathing—

then that I could no longer share my body

in the sleet or even along the rain-bathed diagonal

street that revealed a room for rent in the run-down mauve

of a Norman French façade (its jutting helmet),

then I'd wave, instead, to the lone Salvadoran widow

staring from the window—wave, that is, from my one-fifth-paid-for

car; it was then that the sky was hung

in sulfurous peach, hung in murky scarves or nylon,

slightly but distinctly light;

then that I could not share my gray face,

that I let my mouth go slack and, barefoot,

crossed the wet cement to pee, and then that my blood was horses,

night ones—hooves; my eyelids, for a month—no, more—

itched viciously at night

and below one eye—about the size of a piece of mica

no longer reflecting—then that a patch grew red.

It was then that the six Minervas rose like a Beat hallucination—

open-eyed, yet pupil-less, in the way of certain Roman statues,

standing over twelve-foot tall at the base of Carondelet & Coronado;

then that—just to sample some final, remaining irony—the wisteria,

nearly completely dead on one side of my courtyard, exploded

into maybe 80 purple, graceful blooms in the sudden sun, and the

sodden eucalyptus held up twelve new leaves as the faded paper of its earlier coins began to fall.

And it was then—right then (as the six, the leather, saddles,

wooden slatted cider press, the old piano found their way to storage;

copper tub to salvage; a few bicycles to trash)—then that the

rumpled laundry festered, thrown, unfolded, on the sofa;

then that the dust collected; then that I gave up making—

even trying to make—the bed; then that the dishes gathered

in the sink until they broke; then that there was no further point

in hiding. And it was then, as always at that time of year, that jasmine

laced the chilling air, scumbling even numbness—

even nests of panic, fear.

Its sweetness undermined resolve. Its scent undid the winter.

It was sunny, 47. It was winter, 32.

Padlocks shut the seven doors.

It was all night, then.

NIGHT TEXT

Let's imagine I'm translating something to you—
you, asleep, or sleepless or naming
that third place—between—

with the tips of your tapering fingers—

I don't know the language.
It bends.

In the mind—in that strangely shared chamber—
that is, I mean, in your hands,

where you show me those scenes of confusion and flight
with such intimacy, and don't know it—

even *sans* color, *sans* liquor, *sans* shape,
we are twins. Fraternal. Unknown.

The moon, invasive, huge,
lunging in through the windows,
makes no exceptions—

It's true: it will never happen / you'd be surprised.

ENCLAVE

It's as if you're looking for a restaurant you've been to in a dream—across from the oldest building in town, which you've misconstrued as an inn (it's really a Mission). And instead, you find another restaurant and another—this one Italian, this one ice cream or gelato—honey & lavender, ginger glacé. And the streets are full of drinking, of stares, of the noise of the dark and the music of bands spilling into the streets. Blocks and blocks. You keep looking.

Yes, it's near the end of something—of traffic—the end of the heart of downtown, so near the end that if you were driving, well, you could actually park: no one stays at the Mission at night.

You walk until you recognize the context, even the brick— left raw and unfinished—of the walls, the pendants hung like charms—but the hostess tells you the place you're hoping to find changed hands one month before, and it's now more like a coffeehouse—specials scrawled in chalk on the board, a deli to the side stacked with bottles and cheese.

You're reminded that your timing, never great, feels more like fate—but now you want to return to the restaurant in an *actual* dream, just a café near a reservoir on an edge of town that doesn't exist, where you showed up by chance around noon after leaving a classroom. You want to return because the one you still love had happened to walk in.

And as he recalls it, there was a little room just above—he was sure you'd been there together one night or you'd lived there together, a little apartment. Both of you want to go back. And neither of you can recall even one of its features.

ODE WITH A MOAN IN THE MIDDLE

Everyone stayed safe in the closed mouth,
the tamed / the ironed hair, the well-made
image, cage of no breath, the demure. I did, too.

What had my body become but a scaffold
for work, for holding down lies?

For depriving myself of the truth.

So unlike that poet/priestess photo on the web:
Buddhist shaman in her shaolin, such bright red, that robe—

arms outstretched, her voice outstretched, some tonal jujitsu
so intense the camera records her as a blur: yelling or almost yelling

near-nonstop and it's not that I yell
but that, midsummer, in some act of half-illegal and untethered grace,

I realize I have actually loved. And it's like some layer of skin rips off—

final and fast as a car door pulling off the whole front of my body—
flung off, in the genius wind. Air gets in. And everything in it:

chime-rustle, wind-slip of leaves, whole sashes: trees.
Every glance of light, each slant of the sun's illusory movement—

or rather the real, the actual movement of the earth.

We have made our own containers, cages. They agree
with the necessary boundaries, the conventions.

But even the moon refuses to stay halved
and how can I ban the moon?

Woke up feeling you near, somehow.

Wanted to hold you close in this intimate gray,
dust the darklings off your shoulders. Heal you.

By autumn, air and light so perfectly in balance I can feel a texture—
I could wade through equipoise with you.

The light right now, hitting the low eucalyptus leaves . . .

there's a gentle demand in that light: it wants to be shared.

Night like tulips—
so much opening to you.

Then that dream of waking to your hands—
somehow, you've slipped in.

How you kneel above my waking body on the bed.
How my body turns.

As though your face is in front of me. Right in front of me.

And how do I know, in that other dream: the large house is the wrong house.
I choose the smaller one, the one with "character."

Once I begged for no ring, just to feel your skin, but now I'd wear one
just to get the world off my back.

Even if I touch your skin only in dreams.

Even if it's time to live in a forest, barefoot, like that famous German poet—
gathering mushrooms quickly, throwing them into a pile on the table,

telling us why and how and when they'll change color,
all their stories, their mythologies, their tastes.

Even if my lovers are the trees.

Love, I'll oboe the low long round slow sound for you, oh you—

and I'd do any, anything to loosen my tongue.

BEFORE US

There is a mauve photographic bowl of rain

        —though some would say a cup

A sultry plague before the fandango of alleys

An armament / arm / armband tossed into the gray / the grim Corvette

        at the rehearsal of velour and anise / ankle / anklet

A muzzle of parched starlings sleeping like geckos / geishas / geese

            just lounging

        after the Sabbath of compromised kilt / kin / kiln

(I'm certain about the alleys and the alliances)

(I'm certain of the colour, of the bowl)

And did I mention that huddle of parrots? Yes. Five, green.

          Clustered near the beige of the third-floor windows.

After the honcho / the hole, the whole damn holiday opens

        and the dam spills into the castanets of the waiting hand.

And it's here the maraca ticks like a rattlesnake on a short leash.

(I'm certain of the Geiger counter, the saber /

        the stomping / the sticking.)

And the compensation—it's worthwhile.

There's a moan in the attic, and one in the basement,

A twisting / tweaking / twerking in the den.

To be clear—did I say that the bowl is the size of a valley?

And did I mention this rush is the colour of mauve?

        (As the rehearsal-velour deliquesces to velvet—

      velvet dissolving into the smooth vernacular of fur . . .)

There's a cat / a catch in the breath at the edge of the bed in the lush

      hush of morning,

a slant / a sliver / a sip of new light in the palms.

I'm certain of the armature of nothing . . .

as I'm certain that the husk has cracked, its scraps concussed.

There's a flamenco that rustles the edges of rust and of dusk and of morning,

that rattles the dust from the corridors of musk:

      this is its cusp

(as the licorice Pernods, as socks bloom into paisley stockings,

      as dawn's viridian muddle of leaves becomes a nest of trust

      and armbands / guns are garters—inveterate, seated deep,

I'm certain of the moaning, the anemone, the memory,

the tangle and the tango and the glow—

as I'm certain of the shade, of this blueberry-vermillion.

And of the green parrots, I am certain.

Certain.)

THE HART

—*And I to you of a white goat . . .*

(Sappho, tr. Carson)

And so I imagined the way we'd come across him there,
                              the creature—
gazing at us squarely, loosely chained
—that palimpsest of horn
a singular, curling pentimento—
his throne, a bed of rosemary and bracken
                    and birdlime.
It will not surprise you that he caught us staring—
                or that this was the way he simply caught us.
You will remember—I'm certain—how he wore his crown:
like a cuff.
There was the way his hooves were split
                    and the way he opened time.
We had to notice that the sky of his neck
was golden: a collar:
                how it blended perfectly
into the metal expanse of light.
Sound was the water flowing from the fountain—
                              steady sound.
Runes had fallen like petals
                        from the roses.
You will, of course, receive this
                    (already know it).
Mood rang through the moon—
                an oval in daylight,
                            sinking slow.
This is realism.
Under the fragrant rosemary.
The fog opens, closes.
We live inside these hills.

CIRCLE

Seven days of weeping drown eleven years of being wrong—
and now, at dawn, steam rises off the lake.

You slumber in a penumbra of anesthesia
as I kayak toward the lily pads, their petals reaching up like fingers

into the ceremony of our speaking, once again,
as we once did. Lichen hangs in loose black beards;

and you turn your head—I sense this—on a city pillow
as a peacock walks across the lane

from the yard of the house I grew up in
toward the house where my grandparents once lived.

In a field, a farmers' market: I buy feathers for my earlobes—
feathers I will wear for you, as my body kneels again

in what I've come to recognize as prayer.

GIRL STANDING WITH DEATH BY THE SEA

First, there was rain.
Or the surface was scratched.

It was a long distance from green
to green.

Death was so quiet,
so patient.

Perhaps there had been trees.
Living ones.

Or maybe really just rain.
Or scratches.

It reminded her of standing on top of a hill
and looking down at the city trailing below.

No city, though.

Maybe, in the distance, a sail
or a buoy.

Or a sprinkle of stars, recessed
in that intaglio of green.

And a road, curving along the coastline,
but vacant.

It's so different
from standing on the footbridge

with girlfriends, or cousins,
looking out at the noon lake

or turning around at sunset, removing a hat.
Letting the lake go black.

(In another version, the halo was red—
there was a halo in that version.

It covered her head like a hairband
but she was alone.)

She stands, looking out, until dawn
until the greens are mild

shades of blue, and indigo
is the only place that death might be

—or stone—

nothing but a squiggle,
a puzzle piece.

Stationary, somehow.
In little bursts of wind.

It moves like a wet shadow.
If it moves.

Or now it's dark, her hair is longer,
she carries a tambourine

of yellow roses, and death
is only herself, older, and then much older.

The one in the middle—that self—opens her legs in a V,
naked, clasps her hands behind her head—

but she, the sea-looker-she, looks out at the sea.
Feels them, standing behind her.

She has never seen her own exposure, though she feels it.
When she finally sees it—its strangeness, her own—

well, I tell you, I can't explain why,
but it makes her radiant.

Even when everything goes to woodcut white and black,
she stands on a road
and, behind her, it is not death, but a woman with hair—
herself—and skin. And brows. A woman fully exposed

and her dark-clad companion—night, herself.

Or no—the only color now is the palest blue
of water strafed with cloud

and she stands on the black sand before dawn
in her long pale dress and the frothy, possessed black

waves must be wetting her feet and behind her

a figure approaches—a man?
We see them from behind.

She does not yet hear him.

In her private future red bedchamber,
in her long dark confusion of hair,

there is no shame.

Yes—a man
and her three selves

as she stands in ochre fog
looking out to the sea.

Her hair spills back
into cloud into branch

she is almost a ghost
he clutches his heart

or maybe just his pocket
the moon reflects in the shape of a lingam

not a pearl—all the way down the water
it makes the road larger, pale and wide

with light until we see her turn away
from the water

and now the reflection, long as the dark the rising
dark of the trees—

it is before, just before, they touch.
Death sits silently by

in another version.

There are so many versions.

No, she was never alone.

Hey, lover. Hey lover, lover, lover. . .

PANDORA'S BOX

waited, meanwhile, on a chest. Opened easily. There was a place for a key
to go—a lock—but no key, no need. In it—a candle, black wick; a paper
towel, folded twice, stained by a thumb; a picture, gray tones only—lovers,
say, but as though their edges were nothing but strands of lit candles, lit in
the dark, where lines would be, or lit like circuses or summer courtyards,
little pods of round electricity hinting at the folds of their clothes, the places
where a dimple, a mouth, would be, as though you could pull on one end
and, like a necklace of candles, every defining curve of face, of nape, of the
cut of a jacket would pull into one set of beads to be thrown this way and
that, uninterrupted—not chaos, you see, but joy mistaking itself for chaos in
unintelligible pathways of folding and unfolding change—just close the lid
and you'll notice the darkness of the flowers the box is resting on and, just to
the left, baskets in baskets of straw in heavy, engraved brass pots, where you
can see the way the lion spins around, snarling at the rising python of his own
tail. And just to the left, a crane, still, prey in its beak. And the vines outside
have sprung into tendrils leaping above the paths, embracing, reaching. Their
leaves, bigger than hands, hold fresh droplets like new jewels. And the crane's
beak is open. Suspended.

BRIDE, RUNNING

But it's her way, always, to find burrs caught in her hair, dead pine needles, even today, even, in this endlessness of tulle and lawn-soiled shoes, satin, snail-trail of mascara—and nothing is wrong. Nothing. Nothing except that the planets are off, colliding, turning day into eclipse, and no matter how she runs, she can never seem to make it, like a borrowed horse, to the end of the lawn—the veil streaming behind her in some labyrinth of wind, tiny enough, kicked up by the planets, until the veil and the tulle are as long as the lawn, as long as a lung—one mouthful, diaphanous breath—that stops only when her fingers touch the electric sheath of sky.

BEGINNER'S DAYBOOK

In this garret-muck: puzzling / parsing / purring, scent-spellbound,

     blank / blaring / blazing / bleak,

A green-grey corpus / corpse / corona-dip directs, penetrates,

     all simmer-silt silver.

The mutant music endures / endows, cistern by cistern, citadel by citadel,

A wheel / a whale of sister, nearly too deep to brim.

Hijacked from your frostwork, magician,

You multiply (muffled) / mull within this marabou-brew, this hocus-pocus,

My heaven heavy with your force, your sixth sense, your storm.

A rambling tremble—gossamer—drones / drops / drowses its

Prairies / its praises—drafty, dreamy, drawn

By these local boulders, orchestral and regal.

Even anxiety nourishes the heart / the hearth, this heat

Prankish as kismet, downright preachy, a kind of

Plea to faze fear. Dear ear / dear earth: a prayer to kiss—no albatross,

Rigid—is right. In this parlance of kirsch, of Campari,

Here is the question no mourning can contrive—

     all dazzled flight, dazed parlor—

In bushes / burials native as fir / fire, somber / somnolent beginnings

Kindle hues / kill hubris among the graves / the gravity—all gratitude, all gravy.

I shadow each facet, shake the fabric, fact

A hollow holograph, a holy muddle and meld.

The fugitive brightness of this ebony 8-ball

Corrals / corrects me in this summer suite, its suitcase of sulfur

A sulky rotisserie, sweet rotunda.

The quest, begun, begs, begets this dance, flirtation, masking,

As I massacre your wit

To query, to master the witchcraft

Of your yesteryear, your Yew.

A MIRROR OF LEAVES

Even now, I draw you toward me—

Even as the black mold furs the ceiling,

Spanish moss hanging abruptly from the walls,

Draping across the furniture—that Rococo fauteuil and my settee—

In dry organic antimacassars and ratty doily strands

While the edges of the Aubusson carpet, still beneath us, are sipped—

By silverfish and rug beetles and moths and the curtains

Blow into the room, along with the graying leaves of autumn,

Already dead, already light as termites, thin as ash—

And still, your chest is an open door

And birds fly out

Of the vaulted ceiling of your cathedral heart

Like red origami

And tiny white—fly, they fly into the wild air

Of the room as you tiptoe toward me

In your gray mime, like a shadow

As alive as trees

While I gently pull on the long green strand of yarn

As it gathers into a ball

I can hold in my hand, and some would say

I cry red tears or that

My entire chest is as red as my waist-length uncut hair

And that it seems I can only stare straight ahead as I weep

And pull your open heart

Toward mine, even as this island of wool below us

Diminishes as I perch my stool upon it,

Oblivious to the ragged, shrinking edges,

As the invisible choir of insects

Erodes the original design.

And some would say: so focused am I on the wool in my hand

That I don't even notice the growing devastation

Of the room

But I must tell you

—And you can see this for yourself if you look closely—

That the lines descending from my eyes are not tears, no,

Or even blood—not now—

But merely the last of the remaining gold leaf

Etched into these walls in the 18th century

In another climate—

Barely visible now: a blanched, infested background.

And others do not recognize or know, I guess,

The way the skin can rouge in pleasure—

But mine always does—

And though I know I'm facing the other direction

And shouldn't be able to see this,

If you look yourself, you'll find

That the mirror above the fireplace clearly reflects

The gathering clouds that have entered the room

In a gusty rush of nimbus further darkening the chalky

Charcoal look of the crown moldings

And below the mantel, where the fire should be,

Or at least a screen: a massive nest of webs.

Yet even as everything around us grows gradually

Colourless and intermittently devoured

I can feel you coming toward me, though I can't yet see

The exact features of your face. Your step is light;

Your balance precise and honed as a wooden marionette

Freed of all strings, yet—miraculously—choosing to keep in your heart

This one bit of yarn

As I hold and roll the other end

And as I hand you, finally, this small green ball—

This homespun ball of my waiting—

A bird will fly out of your chest into mine,

And the joined cathedral of our twinned hearts

Will be our sanctuary—sanctuary enough—

Vast enough, unending—

And as this infusion of color you've given me

As I have welcomed you,

Even though the room itself grows nearly tarnished, leached

Of hue, drawn down

To a bleached-out play of values and some drafty chiaroscuro

While the weather and bugs peel the paint and even silently lick

The stains from the corners of the wood and burrow through the cornices—

As this color you've managed to preserve in me

—At some sacrifice to yours, I'd say—seeps back now,

Also, into you,

And my gaze shifts from the task of attending to this yarn

To the proper study of your features—

Because, finally, home is simply an article of faith,

An article of mirror; of mirroring—

As your features become clearer, light unbends

The chambers and the hallways of the cathedral

In which it's as though we've really always lived—

And, even now, can't fathom.

And even in this moment of a room's final unraveling,

This one's no illusion

As it opens into the new, unfolding architecture of our future—

Solid and unfinalfied, unformed.

*

SOFT ACTION

It would be like lips—
pale, orchid, fading
into a white sky—
a bird, the crease,
the silhouette—
gradually disappearing
as a curve of gray,
a pencil mark—
mistake.

Opal—contracting
like a jellyfish
or veil—a skull—
a khaki batwing
folding
into night. An orb,
a bowl for snow, for gathering
blue—a moment
like a cape.

Or like a poppy—imagined
water
color against an equal
wash of brown
—say, dirt—soft
edges, hushed
cloud from the window
of a plane—lush,
bituminous and red.

Or a fading field—a plum,
your scapula—
irrigated
from the center, in a circle,
full of winter
wheat. Moving
into ochre
like a buried wing.
A blade.

IS DROWNING UPSIDE DOWN IN STARS

Because your skirt flew up reversing gravity

Constellations lace you loose as jewels as these rare bijoux

Dream of weightless arms of fins in backstroke flow

Elegantly awkward in your improv

Floating through abandoned weeds in humid déjà vu

Grass just wet with dew in barefoot midnight

He lifts you in the dark as you turn together under stars

Is the clover the stars are the stars the clover

Lap to rest his head to see Arcturus through the leaves o

Morgan Street for miles no thought of noon

Never will hordes of moths attack his hands if you hold them

Past the cemetery lit by his firefly lantern book

Questions settle into skin no longer a mirage

Slip out the door of your own soiree with him who was he with

Twenty-first solstice brand-new birthday-body summer-singing

Under the leaves his eyes are enough

Virtuoso he'll say *my dear virtuoso is it strange to say I'm proud of thee*

⁓

Walk past the edges of town to the place where the night is curved

⁓

You need to take yourself seriously   Decades to absorb

⁓

Zodiac is cousin of the clover the alfalfa

⁓

After midnight when the field becomes a fleeting waltz

⁓

X-ray your heart and you'll find the dogwood the redbud

NOCTURNE ~
IN THE LATE GABARDINE OF THE TREES

It's as though the bed is floating

On a river   at dawn

And the water is singing
As the air sang

When their bodies finally united
And a strand of ribbon coiled around their feet—

Wrapping them together in a silken bobbin—

As the voices hummed around them
Like a choir of women, rapt in chant.

Just as the fire of their kissing
Rose in languid curls of gold,

The mist rises off the water

In the slow amber light
Of a lantern

ON THE 10 EDGES OF MY KNOWING

There is a circle at the top, reddening with her nipple

It is not the cliché but the explanation of the cliché

All origin, all rouge

———————————————

Satin & iridescence are close—

a pale blue satin, pale & ivory

oyster & its shell

———————————————

They found it again, hunched over the sink

Same as chapter 1

———————————————

Marzipan: a copy of a copy of a copy

———————————————

Is a distant cousin, a metaphor of fruit

———————————————

like a tiny ballet shoe

All satin

———————————————

This is where the angel-wings

sprout into the bed

The shoulder blades—

That trust place on the neck

In drifts, like lamps?

like lamplights

---

then the ripples—the white light

rippling surfaces of light

---

while walking

a kind of gold translucence

I had thought it would go on

In the ripening winter,

CYPRESS-ADJACENT

It's only after you compliment me on my Palmer method—which I've managed to loop across a dozen envelopes or so, as well as a book you've brought for me to sign (though so often now I use my semi-doctor's-scrawl); only after the two of us have been sitting across the table from each other, talking, sharing wine?, laughing over some damn thing I can't recall in this "spacious 2nd floor apartment" I've decided to rent, where the view we both enjoy (from several windows, tall) is "comforting and breezy"—and where I can tell that the space will feel even larger if I can just move one of those narrow dining tables just a little closer to the wall and cover it with a sheet— that I remember you are dead. But it's still before I dash back down the stairs to stop at an ATM on my way to meet the landlady, with my roll of coins, to sign. And now is the moment you give me some advice:

A BREATHING LAKE

Above us, floating in the dark
like opened lanterns—

as the water's onyx sheen
closes to opaque:

lotuses, where stars would be.

How we wanted to eat them
with our eyes.

How we almost did.

So much closer now that we could almost pull them
toward us like austere balloons.

All around, our stillness, our suspension.

THE HIDDEN SPRINGS

The water: clean, cool.
You like to sit on the steps, stick your feet in.

You've even mentioned, in some interview,
that it's your favorite place to sit—

just off the kitchen, in the center of the house,
instead of stairs going down to the basement,
when you open the door:
                                steps down to canals
as though a long cave opens,
lit by sunlight from one point that fans out

into a whole city, like a modern Brugge.
You could spend hours here.

You ask me why I've never asked to come to this place.
I say I've always longed to,
                                but thought it was private—

that it should be a place you'd take me
only if you wanted,
                        not a place that I should ask to see.

And as we sit on your steps with our feet in the water
a "strange deer" walks past—big as a moose
but antlers like an elk, maybe eight points each.

I can't explain the movement, it's so slow—"majestic"
comes to mind, but that's not majestic enough.

I have a feeling for a moment that the elk is God—
a god that we can watch.

I think there's light in the antlers.

Amaranth springs up, as you wonder about Paris—
those purple sprigs begin to sprout

and how did I know it was here that we were
when the water erupted, too, from my center

as you held me close, on your lap.

It's enough, maybe, to know it exists—
to know just once.

May I not be greedy for what was.

RED BATH

It bothers you, the ocean—
        the thousand-thousand surfaces   colliding in cold light,
                the way the water seems unjoined
and distant—
        not because of looking down from this great height,
            but something else.

They've put you in first class.
        You don't feel first class—
                or, really, anything.
But you can't stop thinking—turning over
        and over that online article
about Bonnard, the recent exhibition, and that painting:
                    two lovers—
        one about to be his wife
at the base of the picture,
        facing in, three-quarter profile,
            something else occluded
in the brushstroke, yes,   but brushstroke as execution
           of the same perception darkening
his gaze, much later, in that angular
        and razorlike self-portrait
in the mirror of the bathroom,
        as though shaving   or about to shave.

The other lover, central, is a source of light—

        several alterations later maybe it's grown hard
to identify the exact measurements and colors
        of the eyes—but their effect is unmistakable. Recognized.

        And maybe her hair
was really that bright—more light than pale, more midday
        haystack under sun than moon, her face a ruddy

outdoor-colored hue of pink.

It's her effect

he gets at with his brush, more than her features.

We'd recognize her even
             in an airport, even from the back.
                        Or from the side.
                             Or from a whiff of something emanating
like perfume—not scent, exactly.   Something else.

And as you recall the many tiny shingle-lights of paint
                        and how they pull the feeling of a moment
closer than the canvas, almost like a hologram,

you begin to see more clearly something far below the ocean
             —or its surface—something vaguely red, not bright,
                                        but like the color
of old blood, dried blood—

                                 perhaps an immense encampment
        of kelp   or maybe, after all, *the sea incarnadine*, incarnate

as a low animal, amorphous, bigger than a whale, below the topaz—sea grass?
the water itself?—stretching for miles beneath the troubled, vacant surface
now grown clear or opaline or gray—
                             a vast and transparent collection
from the world's spittoons,
             windowing the lower layer of self.

Some say she shot herself, the blonde—designed the moment, the tableau
for him to see.

Others suggest that when he finally chose, conclusively, she arranged
a far more fluid exit in the bath—

different in tone from the ones he painted, would keep painting
of the chosen, who remained, a constant presence, hovering near doorways

in glances, or profile, or silhouette, or partially

hidden or rearranged in the tub by the clean refractions
of yellows and sea-green blues, her body,
                    some observe, never quite coherent
as body, anatomically adrift,
                        almost melting into the thicker warmth
of the fleshlight of the afternoon,

hard to make out, precisely,

        or cut off above the legs—

            as happens when one is walking casually by an open door,
after cradling, say, in one's hands, a tiny dachshund. like a second beating heart,
    and remembers to look in:
            never vivid.   Never whole.   Never, ever, a ghost.

And you drink the coffee as if
you're drinking coffee, though
you can't make out the taste

                as you wonder how he'd sketch the almost browning sea
        on the napkin, as they say he used to do,
            how the brush would catch the splitting,
untethered
        surfaces in light, this ruffling
  of these almost-iron
            shifting shavings of some giant knife,

                    or the gradual seeping up of those other colors.

REAL STATE

Thou shalt hang thy blankets from a tree

or thou shalt score a gig as a retail doorman on Rodeo

Thou shalt cover thyself with a sheet of clear plastic and kick at the corner of Broadway and 6th, while pedestrians pass

Thou shalt fumble for keys at the end of the night shift, still in scrubs

Thou shalt hang a right in thy pre-owned 911 Carrera

Thou shalt remove all personal belongings from thy cubicle before the end of the business day. Here's a box.

Thou shalt spring for the 27-thousand-dollar beaded gown not far from the Bois d'Argent

Thou shalt prop the mattress against the eucalyptus across the street from the house in escrow, the two-story for lease, and the reno covered in Tyvek

Thou shalt park thine SLK 320 under the sycamore leaves

Thou shalt not be able to light your cigarette in the wind as you sit on the stoop behind the open storefront display of wighead mannequins

It's an economy storage box

Thou shalt pick up the tab on the ornamental 13-thousand-dollar Buddha and that 6K bottle of scotch in the duty-free

Thou shalt dry thy clothes on the guardrail in front of the Walgreen's and Shabu-Shabu

Thou shalt walk with weights in the evening as the sky turns amethyst then amber and the water comes on, inches from the rusty grass

Drive 45 on the boulevard

Thou shalt leave the couch and the plastic plant on the curb at the end of the month

Thou shalt load the Relo Cube for pickup at Glyndon and Vienna

Thou shalt live in the back of a 1950s Buick with shattered glass

You can use the wi-fi at the Starbucks next to the Dollar Loan

Thou might get a construction job on the northern side of the National Rent-A-Fence

Thou shalt put the tents up after the shoppers leave

Thou shalt no longer be able to afford the unpermitted room within earshot of gunshot and helicopter

Thou shalt "join the 17 million readers who have fallen"

Thou shalt try to sleep in the late afternoon at the base of a streetlamp on the hidden side of a Shell in the Marina

Thou shalt lose thy shirt selling armor, rugs, and chandeliers

No Parking Any Time

Thou shalt stick two signs in the lawn: "house for lease" and "tutoring"

Thou shalt check the stats on the listings from the last six days

Thou shalt organize thy belongings carefully under the overpass

Thou shalt not vacate the premises without giving a 30-day notice

Thou shalt guard the tents at Venice & Globe

Open door policy

Thou shalt not sleep except upon a concrete floor

OFF H'WOOD BLVD.

Someone had pinned a dollar to the wall
But nobody took it.

Someone bent elbows to pay the cashier
And someone bent elbows to throw out the trash,

Or to drop the used glasses
In gray dishwater.

Their backs facing.
Only three feet away.

And it was almost as easy to think of it as a confession booth
As a bar—

The bare turn of the back of the knee,
The glint of a cross on a neck chain.

Hers. His. Or maybe
She was a waitress, or barmaid,

While he was bussing the tables.
The apron over the mini-skirt,

The long hair pulled into a bun.
Call her Ms. Stella Artois.

Call him Racer Peroni,
Startled, almost upset to see you coming

Toward him, as if the camera were really a gun,
As if his glasses themselves would look right through you—

And they do, while cross-lit above the fake marble,
She could almost be a future pietà

Waiting to receive her customer's order.
Waiting. About to deliver.

IT IS NOT A BRIDGE

The bed   red   wood   with scrolls   —along the side, black ink—

the bed   or the coffin   above the river—   the water filled with bats

         —or birds—

I stand on it—   on top of the red   wood   bed   above the river

in wind—   my hair—long, black—   and all of the layers of my clothes—

swirling in wind like some cubist kimono   —the swirling squares of my robes

and maybe the blankets   I am now standing in   as I raise my white sword—

my sword, my reed   —my quill—   long   white   yellow

—as I raise my long sword   toward the fish   above my head

riding my sleeve   like a sleigh, like a basket—   riding my sleeve

like a silk bassinette   —that whiskerfish   ready to jump in the water

before I fall   before I strike—

MUNCH IS SCREAMING NOW
FROM MANY ANGLES

Wall of hands / Cave of hands

Apartment of hands /

The bridge / The wavering river / The waving hands

From the Dordogne to Argentina

Rio Pinturas / Brooklyn to Berlin—

                            Stravinsky-percussive

Fingers – Lascaux – As if Munch were invented by Pina —

Shadows hitting the wall - Like Klieg light narratives /

Cueva des los Manos / Finger shadows

Large as bodies / Swarming / Clones / *Les Mouches*

(and the mouth opened) / Opposite of a flashlight / Hands

that begin to cover the ears / that climb the walls /that reach

that want to pound the floor in fists

Over the centuries /
                  Of the apartment

Through the open doorway / The blown-off door

Over the bridge / Before time

Until the sound comes through the air

Infectious—

It was going to be joy—

It was almost joy

Where the door would be, climbing

(really) the walls,

At once, gripping the top of the opening,

Munch is multiple—all the dancers, every dancer

Multiple as rhythm / In the empty apartment.

Dressed for a night out—

And so it echoes.

Echoes up through decades, through the whistling tubes,

through pipes. There is no need for furniture

because the sound is the furniture.

The furniture is sound.

The furniture is the future.

The future is not sound.

Munch is a fly on the wall in a black dress,

dress like wings, like mesh and velvet

Dots / Large fly / Is many flies / Long hair pulled back, pulled off the face—

Is a clone / Is many clones / Naked hands, bare feet

Time should lapse

But it doesn't. Time is stuck in its shutter / Time is indiscriminately

Circling / Elastic—

And how did he know / How did she know / How did

She /he know, coming home, on the way home, in the cab, in the dour Uber

(driver barely spoke, playing hip-hop, Mozart, playing Miles)

or the miles of the nearly vacant subway, nearly

pearly—polished shine—in the perfect

thrift shop gown—perfect for another night at

Endswell (for all's well that ends):

Vodka, matcha, seltzer, lemon, thyme—

In our wrecked time—

How did Munch know that the sound would keep going

Right through us

—just as the hands began to cover the ears

(On the bridge / In the empty apartment /

Shadow puppets thrown against

The wall, the cave, the mimeo of time)

As the mouth opened—

AFTER VUILLARD

House is a dappled construct

House is a shadowed land on a small hill

House is before the abundant garden—

The birdlike stems and butterflies

Of flowers pirouetting,

Nearly as large as the windows,

Or leaves like yellow diurnal bats

House is behind the woman in the satin pink kimono,

Face as large as the first floor

House is the tiny gardener,

Head as big as a rose,

Inspecting the hedge

Perspective is filigreed blue shadow

Below the white hibiscus, stamens

Longer than a hand

Is below the dress of light

Across from the curtains

Just to the side of three tercets of windows

Turning red as the roof in the evening sun,

Red as the tallest floribunda

Is the woman with rose-petal hair

In the lattice of shadows, handing—

Is the dark canoe-shaped shadow on the roof

The figure behind the open curtain

The closed cerulean shutters—

Their slightly aged pastel, the texture of their rough wood

The door thrown open

The hot sweet smell of summer-singed pollen

The soft sounds of garments landing on the floor

Is for sale

Is her blue hat

Is the cracked tectonic floor

Is no longer there

Is the sun hitting the pavers, the terraced, dry dirt steps,

All the *fleurs* flying—becoming monarchs—

Perspective is the removed corset

The chair

The thorns

Longer than petals

The flying light

The light flying

Night coming on, to the left

Above the acacia, below the pine

Illuminating the chorus line of genies

Playing their bagpipes

As the cannas and the ultimate dwarf bearded irises

Unfurl, unravel, nearly ragged, vulvic, utterly,

And the whole yard is full of flying things

Abundantly tethered enough to stay in position

For a time

For this moment

The blue, I'm telling you, I can't make out

Though it's closer to larkspur than indigo,

Closer to denim, closer to bamboo

I guess I should be happy

How does it speak?

HUNGER

The slip was not satin, but poppy.

A linen sky gone pale and the long

cascading drapes and walls that same cool white

but the cypress, its fallen needles, the rooftops

were umber, the fence, the beginning of night:

small, invisible cries, and like a wing that wooden

fence grew large with shadow as its shape

entered the window, umber,

amber bulbs exposed below

the flaring black shade,

plump with filament, lit, pendulous

and, it seemed, beginning to rise

as the languor of too many months-without-end—

enforced, unnatural languor—

had gathered, like silk, into the crack of thigh

against bent knee, the seam of fleshy upper arm,

crease of elbow, the mystery

of triangle made by the shade of red cloth fallen high over leg,

the shape the covered nipples made as the breasts splayed

to balance a hand flung backward, out of sight and

into foreshadowing, into the scent of the ganja filling the hallway

—nearly strong as skunk—curving its way below the door and into the room

through the rough-hewn gap where light crept through at night

across the closed face, brow held tight as scar above the nose, kohled eyes focused by a dust mote on the floor or the inner

lip of the terracotta urn.

Scent of sugar, sweat, tobacco seeping through the old pipes,

clinging to the pillows like a second skin.

Galangal nights. Arpeggiated dawn.

Empty Newport pack on the hellstrip.

Mind like ribbons. Leather bangs.

Time beyond girdle, the giving up,

the belly abundant, the giving in,

again, again, again, again, again.

FIELD OF THORNS

He could leave the front door locked for days as the grays pooled in layers shrouding the shocking green, at least finally green after months of cold and gray and dun and smashed-looking grasses and plowed fields, that may or may not have been planted, had sprung into lengthy choruses of emerald, collaged by the deepening greens of nearly blue-black leaves as the sun was revealed, for the moment: as though one could glimpse a sustained chord and its deepening shadow—always/never there.

He could leave the door locked and he would have—had he been more nearly alone, unattended, unserved in these wrecked and exasperant seasons of water, dishevelers, unwilling to fall, these seasons that pull all the will out and force you to lie on the sheets as the bedding slides off, forgetting the pruning shears and the scythes and the clippers on the broad front steps, leaving them unused for days.

He would have, disheveled, had he not had to resort, instead, to the privacy of the glass, of the liquids at hand, the burnished, the burning, the amber, the quelling capacity they still held out against all those inner expanses of gray, exposed, vast, roiling, nearly royal purple to the south or the ore of gunmetal, the shifting steel of a school of dull knives, floating together, west.

Walking under them, under the constantly moving and burgeoning gathering clouds, under the miles of their unpredictable rousing—looking up, disoriented, nearly falling, which would be like resting on something strangely stationary below a constantly changing ceiling—

as surprising as the newly fresh smell of water on dirt, or even near dirt after days of holding back—the wait of it, the way the knuckles begin to swell, the need to pull the clouds out of the body—but to be under them was all ocean, ocean above. Walking could build the fire back, could kindle the flame inside, the flint and the friction, the little light.

He could leave us for days. Longer, at work on the drawings, or longer, alone in the work of making light behind the tapestries, of making marks on pages, finding some color, tangling the wind and the watery gray chill with the stolen dresses of childhood, the rip in the veil, the breaking slate, the buried crab, the stilled lips, the burning bird, the snow, the palms, the stones, the abundant endless heat, the ferocity of our love for him.

THE SINGING

Because the halo has descended
to your hips
               as light
                       on the horizon
the sky around your head
closes in

in green—
         moody muddy green—

and your feet are the size
of small fingers

         somehow on the ground
                   where you stand—
voluminous
        billowing

in a black as soft as clouds

below the flower—

        the bow—

            in your hair

blooming as large as a face

        before the rain
        before the evening

            while the hill is still touching
            your thigh

AT HAWTHORNE BRIDGE

Until a bear arrives, in darkness.

As though the air has gotten into everyone's clothes.
Or the water has. I force myself to look away.

The men walking solo. Staring into the muddy brown,
the towering. That weird sense of Celan.

So many posing below the promised petal canopy.
Uncomfortably damp.

Or that fantasy of too much whiskey.
You know, there are ways.

And I'm close to turning back to lie in the snow. A little too close.
Or I'm shooting a video of my footsteps on the phone. Cellos, violins.
Something like a carnival arrives. And what to call those sounds

weaving from their strings? Black cases open.

But maybe there's another way . . .
my grandfather tumbling rocks in his garage. Until the smooth stones glistened.

Glistened as much as when they were submerged.

Another kind of baptism.
Like water without water.
But with the absolution with the shine.

WOULD NOT HAVE SEEN EACH OTHER FOR YEARS

Jupiter comes. The red whips. Smoke-dusk clouds of mauve.
I am the bass note, the string. You're the finger.

> He says, *Try to get your images*
> *from the inside.   It starts small. Precise:*

the lingering shadow of a ghost web
hangs like lichen, lifted by a fan.

> I tell him it reminds me of Dürer's
> last self-portrait: that's how his face looks.

Toward the same magnet: birds fall like ash,
untouchable through blackening trees, carnelian.

> Here's an image: flying back from his face;
> what will it look like from inside?

Fire-skies of ruby, skies of garnet.
Birds, like falling paper, twirl down

> and that's how you face it. It starts small. Precise.
> I tell him it reminds me of Dürer's

birds like ash, falling.

KAIROS AT NIGHT

It seems to be a hammer
until I pick it up—

on the asphalt, white on black: a broken racket,
at the rim, says *Service.*

You hurl it, in the dark,
across the field, over the net.

It bounces once. There are no strings.
We are not even.

In the darkness, clover is a constellation.
After this much wet grass,
my feet are so cold, they forget.

You lift me to the stars.
But I am heavy, like a lamb

in the water. The wool gathers
again its weight
in river.

The light does to the trees
what the leaves do
to the stars.

Your head is in my lap.
It is lighter than I thought.

Your eyes, the stars
are leaving.
Clover is a consolation.

Take what you're given,
and give to whatever you take.
Don't complain.

I know you by the way your eyes squint through the leaves.
All of them.

REHEARSAL FOR ENDING

Feathers—
or birds, or leaves

fell slowly into the snow
among the dark thin hounds

and their hunters,
obscuring the wet bark torsos

of the trees,
larger

even than the black-clad
skaters on celadon

ponds, grim as the
morning sky

and melting as,
seconds later,

snow—I'm sure—was floating up—
flakes or white feathers

losing their scant
gravity

as the ice began to burn
along the edges

and the drifts of tulle,
veiling the long grass—

already slowed, elongated—
tangled in muddy clouds of web

as Mahler appeared—
I think it was Mahler

—or something had happened to the air,

echoing the distance among those same
increasing shades of green, in notes

or in what trembles—

something else, something far apart

as the roiling gray of a fishtail-
braided cloud, years

and seconds later

in that pentimento of rain,
grainy and dark

and darkening the distances of green
waters and murky fields

until it seems barely possible to make out
the few abandoned fishing boats

and almost impossible to tell
whether the two tall stalks

are cut-off sails
or the edges of self-pruning cottonwoods

that have grown, in confusing weathers,
up through salt

and through the teal and emerald of
the slippery reeds of shore toward the roiling gray corn

of the clouds in their horizontal twisting above shards of wall
below. And then white moths,

like motes, floating into the star-dark sky,
just as after the box is opened and things fly out

some of them are still alive, and light,
even as the sail-cloak darkens over the body

and the lover extends the fingers again toward the wound, and tries,
and cannot stand.

DRAFT

How could it come to you, again, from such a past
       Or, as later, rain pelting the hut
And you don't question them—
       The new, temporary ditches lining the thresholds
       These rushes—kettle pennies clattering skylights
            Or now
A neutral silence, just ringing
       Or an engine tracing the movement of a passing plane
                 An itching hand
A start

How does it translate
       The vague sounds of distant tires
       A recognition: stiffness in the neck
And a residue of truffle honey on goat cheese saved from a party
       The old red, or the muscular sable
Like a cat, offering its tail
          Or the little trickle in the body waking itself up
And tired eyes
As though one could hear
       The sound of the dark

IN THE LATE GABARDINE OF THE TREES
~ CADENZA

One could be ravenous. One could find small bones in the chicken,

Find them by feel, just in time. One could desire to commemorate

The one eighth of the time spent in the company of pleasure, in the presence

Of desire—or the 1/32nd or 1/132nd or the 1 in

Eleven hundred or so

Or the pure/dark stillness of the trees in fog placed like a group of statues—

Just so—as though their arrangement together

Had long been planned, not grown into;

Or a piece of film

And the sound of a casual Stalinist's piss—

Also his wonder,

His wandering

Into the tall ruins of a church

(Why do I always think of Chernobyl)

That could just as easily be the long-abandoned remains

Of a cooling tower

Or a cave

But just below the cool and concrete wall

The remnants of a painted face

As big as a body—

One could say *I want for you to close your eyes*

And listen. Just listen.

What I have given.

What I have given up.

What I would give—

And the way we just seemed to walk into the middle of something

Already happening.

Incidental witnesses

Recording:

      A sweater slipped on backwards

      Label touching chest above the breastbone

      Dirt gathered around the edge of a nail

      Or the way skin feels when it hasn't been washed—

Or the man takes off his cap

As if about to look in the mirror

And it's 1949

But he meets the gaze, instead, of those gigantic, distant eyes—

Translucent—and how do they do that,

Painted, as they are, on stone—

Of the face still visible on the wall,

Welcoming, dispassionate,

Just as a helicopter circles

60, 70 years away at the edge of a distant continent.

Finally, late winter comes.

We can almost feel the mud

Giving under the tires of the open-canvas jeep

In graytones in grayscale

As the road splits.

One could walk away.

One could.

One could turn back.

Because you sometimes swear.

You say *I am fucked. You are fucked.*

He/she/it/they/ is/are fucked.

We are.

Or the way Stalin's face unfurls.

Gigantic backdrop.

Facing no one.

Deserted trees.

Or, near sunset, in the empty wheat field

And its single tree—

LETTER ALMOST SENT

You won't like this.

                             Maybe you won't want it.

I'm lying here in the dark with my burning candle—

                                           otherwise, it's still. I tried again
not to think of you today.

It was so cold, even though it's still September, that I had to wear two coats.
It wasn't quite enough.

By nightfall, it was brisk—leaves already golden,
fallen, wet.

          We walked quickly, my friend and I, from the parking lot

to the symphony. I made it nearly to the end of the Rimsky-Korsakov—

all the way to that crescendo and quickening, that cymbal crash—

   and then

         in the place where things go suddenly quiet, but alive—

into that barely audible, sustained, pianissimo pulsing

                                 —lingering—

exactly like it always is when we're together, after—

                       holding each other—

                            exactly like this

but in sound.

         You must listen.

How could it have been composed without this private knowledge—

   this experience?

It was shocking.   To understand this.   I can smell your skin.

They say he used to compose while walking along the footbridges

         between the bulrushes and bending willows,

                              the gardens and the lake.

The Germans leveled the summer house where he wrote it.

I so hope you're ok.

Don't worry.   I know nothing can happen.

Though this feels so strange.

Can't not think of you at night in the ice palace of Varykeno

                              (so cliché, I know)—
crystalline, deserted, filled with snow—

         even though we know it wasn't constructed on the steppe,

but in a studio lot near Madrid,
                    not far from the airport—

the ice made out of cellophane
                    and paraffin;

the snow a mix of aspirin powder and soap flakes

                    —just as hard to walk through as real snow:

Not ours to enter.

      And anyway, it doesn't exist.

            Forgive me.

PS. My brother and I spent several hours

            trimming the apple trees in the yard

as sunset flecked its pink and orange against gray.

          We caught it just in time.

NOTES

"The Sleeping Arrows": borrowed phrase from Jean Valentine's "The River at Wolf"

"Before Us": after K. Fagan Grandinetti

"The Hart": after The Wilton Diptych, with borrowed phrase from H. Crane

"Girl Standing With Death by the Sea": after Munch

"Bride, Running": after von Trier

"Beginner's Notebook": after Plath

"A Mirror of Leaves": after Remedios Varo's "Les Feuilles Morte"

"Soft Action": after a discontinued screen-saver

"Is Drowning Upside Down in Stars": after Lecuyer, after F. Wright

"Nocturne ~ In the Late Gabardine of the Trees": after Klimt

"A Breathing Lake": after Ushio Amagatsu's "Kagemi—Beyond the Metaphors of Mirrors," performed by the Sankai Juku company

"Cypress-Adjacent": for Ralph Angel, late 2020, i.m.

"Red Bath": after Bonnard; with borrowed phrase from Shakespeare's *Macbeth*

"Real State": after Moses, Hockney, Bosch

"Off H'wood Blvd.": after a photo by Alexis Rhone Fancher

"It Is Not a Bridge": after a detail from the *Saddharmadarikasutra*, 13th century handscroll

"Munch Is Screaming Now from Every Angle": after Kristin Lodoen; after Munch

"After Vuillard": after Vuillard's "Garden at Vaucresson"

"Hunger": after Tamara de Lempicka

"Field of Thorns": after C. Bronte and Jean Rhys

"The Singing": after Goya's "The Marchioness of Las Mercedes," about 1798

"Would Not Have Seen Each Other for Years": after Jericho Brown

"Kairos at Night": after F. Wright

"Rehearsal for Ending": after Brueghel, Freidrich, Wagner, von Trier

"Draft": after Reverdy

"In the Late Gabardine of the Trees ~ Cadenza": after Pawlikowski's *Cold War*

"Letter Almost Sent": after Rimsky-Korsakov's *Scheharazade*, after Pasternak

ACKNOWLEDGMENTS

Many thanks to the editors and publishers of these journals and anthologies, where the following first appeared, sometimes in differing versions:

Air/Light: "Hunger," "Red Bath," "It Is Not a Bridge," and "The Hart"
Al-khemia Poetica: "Kairos at Night"
Anacapa Review: "The Singing"
Askew: "Enclave"
Blackbird: "Soft Action" and "The Glass Sonata"
Cultural Daily: "Ode With a Moan in the Middle"
Fanzine: "Girl Standing With Death by the Sea"
FIELD: "Night Text," "Circle," and "Before Us"
Hotel Amerika: "A Mirror of Leaves"
Levure Litteraire: "Bride, Running"
Manoa: "Rehearsal for Ending"
Moria: "A Breathing Lake"
Poetry Daily: "Night Text"
Poetry International Online: "The Hidden Springs"
Pool: "On the 10 edges of my knowing"
Pratik – The Ghosts of Paradise: "Real State" and "Off H'wood Blvd."
Spillway: "Pandora's Box"
TELEPHONE: "Munch Is Screaming Now from Many Angles"
The International Literary Quarterly: "Is Drowning Upside Down in Stars," "Real State," "Would Not Have Seen Each Other for Years," "At Hawthorne Bridge," "Draft"
The Laurel Review: "Cypress-Adjacent"
The Taos Journal of International Poetry & Art: "The Sleeping Arrows"
Tupelo Quarterly: "After Vuillard," "Beginner's Daybook," "In the Late Gabardine of the Trees ~ Cadenza"
VerseVille: "Nocturne ~ In the Late Gabardine of the Trees"

"Letter Almost Sent" is included in the anthology *Written Here,* from the Community of Writers. "Field of Thorns" appears in *Gondal Heights: A Bronte Tribute Anthology.* "Night Text" and "Girl Standing With Death by the Sea" were also anthologized in *Angle of Reflection* (Arctos Press). "Song of the Broken Dice" appears in the anthology *Beat Not Beat* (Moon Tide Press). "Munch is Screaming Now from Many Angles" was initially developed for the virtual installation *TELEPHONE—a game of art whispered around the world*, and also selected for the accompanying print volume *TELEPHONE—Writings* (Crosstown Press). "Rehearsal for Ending" is one of five poems, from this and earlier collections, selected by Katerina Zacharia for the song cycle "Identity Had Gone," composed by Kostas Rekleitis (Bandcamp). And extra thanks to *Tupelo Quarterly* for featuring an excerpt from this collection, and to *Furious Pure* for publishing a sample of it.

The development of these poems was supported by a residency at Yaddo, a COLA Individual Artist Fellowship from the Los Angeles Department of Cultural Affairs, the Community of Writers in the Olympic Valley, at Palisades Tahoe, California, and a post-grad scholarship from VCFA.

Without whom: love and enduring gratitude to my poet pals in The Monday Night Poetry Posse (the Venice Salon) and The Bridge Poets and, for mentoring and inspiration, David Wojahn and David St. John. Special thanks to Forrest Gander, Robert Hass, Sharon Olds, David Tomas Martinez, Jane Miller, and Brenda Hillman for notes on early versions of a group of these poems; to Ellen Bass, Jericho Brown, and Mariano Zaro for prompts that bloomed, and to Betty Thisted for the gift of the symphony. Huge gratitude to all the folks at What Books Press, especially Gail Wronsky, for believing in this book, Kevin Cantwell, for editorial suggestions, and book design wizard Ash Good.

SARAH MACLAY is the author of four previous poetry collections, most recently *The "She" Series: A Venice Correspondence*, a braided collaboration with poet Holaday Mason, as well as three chapbooks and "Fugue States Coming Down the Hall," anthologized in *Scenarios: Scripts to Perform*. Her poetry is also the lyric basis for composer Kostas Rekleitis's classical album of art songs, *Identity Had Gone*. A recipient of *The Tampa Review* Prize for Poetry and a Pushcart Special Mention, and a finalist for the *Blue Lynx Prize*, among other honors, her work has been supported by a Yaddo residency and an Individual Artist Fellowship from the City of Los Angeles. A contributing Book Review Editor of *Poetry International* for a decade and founding artistic director of the gallery-based reading series The 3rd Area, her poems, essays, and criticism have appeared widely in journals and anthologies—among them, *The American Poetry Review*, *FIELD*, *Ploughshares*, *The Writer's Chronicle*, and *The Best American Erotic Poetry: 1800 to the Present*. A Montana native with degrees from Oberlin and Vermont College of Fine Arts, she has taught creative writing and literature and conducted poetry workshops at USC, Beyond Baroque, the Ruskin Art Club, Loyola Marymount University and beyond.

WHAT BOOKS PRESS

AN IMPRINT OF

THE GLASS TABLE

COLLECTIVE

LOS ANGELES

All WHAT BOOKS feature cover art by Los Angeles painter, printmaker, muralist, and theater and performance artist GRONK. A founding member of ASCO, Gronk collaborates with the LA and Santa Fe Operas and the Kronos Quartet. His work is found in the Corcoran, Smithsonian, LACMA, and Riverside Art Museum's Cheech Marin collection.

As a small, independent press, we urge our readers to support independent booksellers. This is easily done on our website by purchasing our books from Bookshop.org.

WHATBOOKSPRESS.COM

2018

Interrupted by the Sea
PAUL LIEBER
POEMS

The Headwaters of Nirvana
BILL MOHR
POEMS

2017

*Gary Oldman Is a Building
You Must Walk Through*
FORREST ROTH
NOVEL

Rhombus and Oval
JESSICA SEQUEIRA
STORIES

Imperfect Pastorals
GAIL WRONSKY
POEMS

2016

The Mysterious Islands
A.W. DEANNUNTIS
STORIES

*The "She" Series:
A Venice Correspondence*
HOLADAY MASON
& SARAH MACLAY
POEMS

Mirage Industries
CAROLIE PARKER
POEMS

2015

*The Balloon Containing
the Water Containing the
Narrative Begins Leaking*
RICH IVES
STORIES

*The Shortest Farewells
Are the Best*
CHUCK ROSENTHAL
& GAIL WRONSKY
LITERARY COLLAGE/PROSE POEMS

2014

It Looks Worse Than I Am
LAURIE BLAUNER
POEMS

They Become Her
REBBECCA BROWN
NOVEL

*The Final Death of Rock-and-
Roll
& Other Stories*
A.W. DEANNUNTIS
STORIES

Perfecta
PATTY SEYBURN
POEMS

2013

Brittle Star
ROD VAL MOORE
NOVEL

Sex Libris
JUDITH TAYLOR
POEMS

Start With A Small Guitar
LYNNE THOMPSON
POEMS

Tomorrow You'll Be One of Us
GAIL WRONSKY,
CHUCK ROSENTHAL
& GRONK
ART/LITERARY COLLAGE/POEMS

2012

*The Mermaid at the Americana
Arms Motel*
A.W. DEANNUNTIS
NOVEL

The Time of Quarantine
KATHARINE HAAKE
NOVEL

Frottage & Even As We Speak
MONA HOUGHTON
NOVELLAS

*West of Eden:
A Life in 21ˢᵗ Century Los Angeles*
CHUCK ROSENTHAL
MAGIC JOURNALISM

2010

Master Siger's Dream
A.W. DEANNUNTIS
NOVEL

Other Countries
RAMÓN GARCÍA
POEMS

A Giant Claw
GRONK
ESSAY BY GAIL WRONSKY
SPANISH TRANSLATION
BY ALICIA PARTNOY
ART

*Coyote O'Donohughe's
History of Texas*
CHUCK ROSENTHAL
NOVEL

So Quick Bright Things
GAIL WRONSKY
BILINGUAL, SPANISH TRANSLATION
BY ALICIA PARTNOY
POEMS

2009

*Bling & Fringe
(The L.A. Poems)*
MOLLY BENDALL &
GAIL WRONSKY
POEMS

April, May, and So On
FRANÇOIS CAMOIN
STORIES

One of Those Russian Novels
KEVIN CANTWELL
POEMS

*The Origin of Stars
& Other Stories*
KATHARINE HAAKE
STORIES

Lizard Dream
KAREN KEVORKIAN
POEMS

*Are We Not There Yet?
Travels in Nepal,
North India, and Bhutan*
CHUCK ROSENTHAL
MAGIC JOURNALISM

WHAT
BOOKS
PRESS

LOS ANGELES